How To Start A
Business In 7 Steps

By Tolga Cakir

My Best Wishes To Jelena
From Tolga Çakir

Published by Black Eagle Publishing Ltd.

Office 34
New House
67-68 Hatton Garden
London
EC1N 8JY
UK

Copyright © 2015 by Tolga Cakir

Hardcover Edition May 2015

Printing:
Ege Reklam Basım Sanatları San. Tic. Ltd. Şti.
Esatpaa Mah. Ziyapaşa Cad. No:4
34704 - Ataşehir / İSTANBUL
Telephone: 0216 470 44 70
Fax: 0216 472 84 05
www. egebasim. com. tr

Printing Certificate Number:

12468

For information about special discounts for bulk purchases please contact
bill@howtostartanonlinebusinessin7steps.com

CONTENTS

BIOGRAPHY

Tolga is a business author and has a background in business information systems. Tolga received his BSc (Honours) degree in Business Information Systems from the University of Leeds Metropolitan. Tolga has consulted many managers, executives, business owners, and entrepreneurs. In addition to being consultant, Tolga spent many years as a journalist and a professional coach. Despite his demanding career, Tolga makes time to be involved with community, and professional organisations. Tolga Cakir lives in London. When Tolga is not working, he likes to travel, take photos and write.

Here is my website www.tolgacakir.com

PLEASE REVIEW!

Reviews make a real difference for authors. If you like this book, please give it a good review on the site where you purchased it! Word of mouth is one of the best kinds of advertising out there and, even if you only do a very short review, know that it is greatly appreciated.

FREE OFFER

Free 30 minutes E-commerce or social media consultancy for your start up for a limited period only. Enter your code at the page 98 where it says "REVIEW: FREE OFFER"

For a free offer, quik sign up at www.howtostartanonlinebusinesssin-7steps.com with your name, email and the code at the page 98 "RE-VIEW: FREE OFER"

www.howtostartanonlinebusinessin7steps.com

RECOMMENDED SERVICES

For transformational coaching, E-commerce and social media consultancy please check

www.howtostartanonlinebusinessin7steps.com

COPYRIGHT NOTICE:

INTRO

Starting an online business is a big undertaking. In order for you to ease this big task for you, this book divides it up into seven logical steps, many of them concentrating on what you need to do once you have your page up and running. Additional information explains the ins and outs of accounting software, buying and selling advertisements on websites and more.

The first steps are always the hardest. Once you're ready, up and running, you'll discover that things become much easier and that being successful on your business is much more than a real dream; this is a real possibility, provided you do things in the right way! The following seven steps constitute what most businesses will need to do:

1. Get a domain
2. Get a website set up
3. Engage in search engine optimization on page
4. Engage in search engine optimization off page
5. Choose paid advertising venues
6. Track your results and returns on investments
7. Be prepared for the everyday, offline elements of doing business

The following information will help to achieve all of these goals.

CHAPTER 1
SETTING UP SHOP

The initial stages in starting up an online business involve, first and foremost, getting your domain and your website ready to go. Getting your domain and website is much easier than it was even five years ago. The main things you'll need to keep in mind are:

- The amount of bandwidth you expect to consume
- Any specialized security features you need on your site (SSL, etc.)
- The amount of server space you need (disk space)
- What type of hosting you need

BANDWIDTH

Bandwidth is not as much consideration as it used to be. Many professional web hosting products come with unlimited bandwidth, which is the best way to go if you believe that you're going to get a lot of traffic. GoDaddy, for instance, offers several packages that have unlimited bandwidth. Always remember, you can always get a cheaper web hosting deal with limited bandwidth and then scale up when your business starts to take off.

SECURITY

Information relating to security is at the end of this chapter. SSL is an essential component and must for every site that takes personal information, including financial information, from customers.

SERVER SPACE

Most web hosts offer unlimited disk space at this point. Remember that website files are tiny, in most cases, so even limited plans should include plenty of space, particularly at startup, and you can then expand this as you need.

WHAT TYPE OF HOSTING?

Because you're starting up a business, free hosting is not an option. It sometimes comes with advertisements included on your pages at the discretion of the web hosting company, and those advertisements may be for competitors. Here are the viable types of web hosting for businesses.

SHARED HOSTING, AKA VIRTUAL HOSTING

The least expensive of the paid options, in most cases, shared hosting means that you share a server with other sites. You cannot access these other sites from your administration panels, nor can the administrators of those other sites access yours. No one on the Internet will be aware that you share server space with other sites. The main advantages with this type of hosting includes good support and low costs. The disadvantages include limited space, less available features and the security risks of sharing your server with other sites.

DEDICATED HOSTING

Dedicated hosting means that you lease your own server over which you have complete control. Having your private server gives you the most power and flexibility. At the same time, having a dedicated hosting is a lot more complicated to administer and manage than virtual hosting. Some dedicated hosting packages come with a barebones server, and you'll have to install all the necessary software—Word Press, Joomla, databases, etc.—from scratch.

Either of these is a viable option. Some businesses may opt to go with the less expensive shared hosting and then graduate to dedicated hosting when traffic and technological demands necessitate the move.

GETTING A DOMAIN NAME

Your domain name is a vital consideration. Ideally, your domain name should match your business name exactly, with no hyphens, though there is some room for creativity here. If company domain name matches your business name that is referred to as a masthead domain. For instance, if your company were named Acme Stuff Co., your masthead domain would be AcmeStuffCo.com.

The ".com," ".net," etc. at the end of domain names is referred to as the Top Level Domain (TLD). Commercial websites should always try to get a dot-com name. A dot-biz name is a viable alternative.

Domain name registration usually covers a year of ownership and can be obtained at prices under $10, in most cases. Some of the most-popular registrars include:

- GoDaddy.com
- 1and1.com
- Enom.com
- NetworkSolutions.com

NOTE: Your domain name registration does not cover your web hosting costs. They are separate products. Some registrars, however, will offer you a free domain name registration together with a new web hosting package. You have to look for these kinds of deals.

You have the option to register your domain anonymously, which allows you to avoid having your contact information used for spam lists. GoDaddy and others offer this service. You can get a rundown on the GoDaddy version of the service here: http://www.godaddy.com/domainaddon/private-registration.aspx

GETTING HOSTING FOR YOUR SITE

Getting web hosting for your site is very easy. All you really have to do is sign up for one of the packages from the provider you intend to use, give billing information and the domain you want to record with the site, and you're just about ready to go. Some considerations you will want to address include:

- Content management system compatibility (WordPress, Joomla!, Drupal, etc.)

- Database resources
- Administration panel
- Preinstalled services

Provided you get the plan that meets all of your requirements in these regards, you should be set up to get started as a new business.

SIMPLE SITES CHECKLIST

For the simplest sites—such as sites that only advertise and promote a business, but that are not eCommerce sites—make sure that your web hosting package includes the following:

- No Webhost-determined advertising
- FTP access
- Content management system platforms as needed
- Databases
- Email addresses
- Mobile Site Compatibility

WORDPRESS

WordPress is a practical type of content management system (CMS) that is very well known and very popular among bloggers. It's an excellent resource for people building their websites. Most web hosts have the platform installed on their servers already, and all you have to do is activate it.

If you intend to use the WordPress platform, which can cut out thousands of dollars in web development costs and give professional results, check this with your web host before you buy a package to see if they have it installed in their system. WordPress uses variety of themes that allow you to customize your site. There are thousands of free themes available, and there are paid themes, as well, which come with more features and support, in most of the cases.

WordPress is one of the most widely known and used content management systems in the world, so it is not at all being unprofessional to use this CMS instead of having your site developed from scratch by a programmer.

COMPLEX SITE CHECKLIST

If you're going the route of dedicated hosting, check for the following:

- Web hosting control panel: cPanel, etc.
- Verify server space
- Technical support options
- Security

SECURITY

SSL (Secure Socket Layer) is a form of security most commonly used to secure transactions involving credit cards, bank accounts and so forth. Another important function of SSL is transferring a great deal of other secure information, such as logins and passwords, in many cases. It doesn't cost much to set up anymore. The cost will vary between hosts, and you'll need to renew this service annually or on another schedule, depending upon your host. A secure page has "HTTPS" in front of the address instead of "HTTP."

If you want the technical info: SSL works with RSA encryption, and this makes it possible for users to exchange information with your servers in a secure way (Downing, Covington, & Maulldin, 2009 p. 454). If you are requesting any type of information from users that must be kept safe from hackers, you need SSL. All eCommerce sites need this.

These cover the basics of getting set up. The next chapter is going to address you promoting the site that you just got started.

CHAPTER 2

PROMOTING YOUR SITE

Getting your site ready, up and running is not particularly difficult these days. Using a CMS such as WordPress makes it very fast and very easy to do. Promoting your site, however, is much more complicated and requires that you develop a working knowledge of SEO, social media promotion and other tools.

SEARCH ENGINE OPTIMIZATION

Search engine optimization involves two main efforts: on page optimization and off page optimization (Fleischner, 2011 p.29). The search engine optimization you do on your page includes things such as:

- Adding meta-tags
- Validating the code on your site
- Choosing appropriate keywords and implementing them accordingly in the right way
- Addressing your demographic's likely search questions

Some sources claim that an on-page optimization is not quite as important as it once was. This is simply because the author of the page has complete control of this effort—including the control required using black-hat SEO tactics. Search engines don't put as much weight as they once did upon meta tags and other parts of the page that people control themselves (Google, Inc., 2009). On the other hand, some experts do recommend that you put some time into meta tags. In short you have no choice, but to make sure that your code is valid, meaning that it conforms to the standards of the World Wide Web Consortium, in order to be sure that the search engines, including Google, can read it (Fleischner, 2011 p. 41). WordPress has features built into it that allow you to fill in meta tags without having to open up the source code files from the site (WordPress.org).

OFF-PAGE OPTIMIZATION

Off-Page optimization is more complicated compared to on page optimization. This type of optimization involves undertaking a concentrated effort to increase the overall popularity of your site on the Internet, thereby increasing the importance of your site in the eyes of the search engines (Fleischner, 2011 p. 85). This effort, importantly, includes getting the Page Rank of your site—a metric used by Google to rank the importance of sites—higher and, of course, making sure your site comes up right at the top in the search engine results for searches that are related to your keywords.

The quality and the ranking of the websites that link to your site are crucial to this effort. You can download a tool for your browser that can allow you to see the page rank of any site: The Google Toolbar. You'll find it located at: http://toolbar.google.com/.

The higher the PageRank, the more desirable a back-link—a link leading to your site from that site—is. Having high-quality sites linking to your own can help you to get listed first on search engines, even among competitors who may have the same keywords and demographic targets that your site has (Fleischner, 2011 p. 86).

Off-page search engine optimization includes many of the areas that this chapter will cover, including blogs, video marketing, article marketing, social media marketing and more.

LOCAL SEO

Local SEO principally involves Google Places, a service from the search engine that allows users to find resources in their local area. Optimizing your page for this service is comprised of two things, one of which you can control and one you cannot.

You can set your Google Places account setup at: https://accounts.google.com/ServiceLogin?

service=lbc&continue=https://www.google.com/local/add%3Fservice%3Dlbc. You have to make sure you fill out as much information as you can on your profile as this is one of the the best ways to get good placement on user searches for local resources. You can add photos of your business and add a very detailed description, among other features. You should fill in everything you possibly can on this profile to get the best results (Fleischner, 2011 p.179).

The second part of optimizing your site for Google Places is, however you have little control over this. The more and better reviews you get on Google Places, the better it is for your site. Encourage your customers and clients to offer a review of your services. Don't pay people to put up phony reviews. Negative reviews amidst positive reviews make it easier for people to take your positive reviews seriously (Fleischner, 2011 p. 179), so don't despair if you get a few negative reviews now and then. If you do have a local outlet, remember that Google itself claims that 97% of consumers use the Internet to find local businesses these days. The Yellow Pages are, in today's world, far less relevant than the Internet in this regard.

The next sections will give details on article marketing and other strategies that you can use to market your site on other Internet sites. Used correctly, they are very capable of creating good results, indeed.

ARTICLE MARKETING

Article marketing is a form of content marketing involving writing articles that are relevant to your website (Wikipedia.org) and getting back-links from those articles to your site.

There are many different sites where you can post articles and get back-links to your site. Remember that Google does consider the quality of the sites that link to yours, so you'll want to keep this in mind when you're choosing sites that you want to post your content on. Always remember that you need to have high-quality content in your articles (Fleischner, 2011 p. 117).

Your articles should be spread out over several different directories, giving you back-links from a variety of different sites. You can write the content yourself but, unless you're a superb writer, it will be better to have the articles professionally written. You can order articles from content writing companies by giving them the subject of the article and the keywords you want included in the context. If you use this technique correctly, you can then promote your site very effectively and can dramatically increase your PageRank (Wikipedia.org).

SOME CONSIDERATIONS FOR ARTICLE MARKETING

- Stuffing keywords—meaning using them too frequently—negatively affects your results from this method
- Low-quality articles will have negative effects on your search engine optimization
- Posting on sites with low PageRank will do less for your PageRank

VIDEO MARKETING

Video marketing is exactly what the name implies: marketing your website through videos posted on the Internet. Video marketing can be a great strategy for promoting your site.

Video marketing oftentimes involves producing videos of special offer included with them, or that have a call to action (Fachini, 2012 p.50). Remember that your video is going to be competing for the attention of viewers in an environment where there are thousands of others that they can watch, so yours had better give them a good reason to pay attention rather than going off to watch something else. Offers and calls to action provide effective ways to make videos more engaging.

Effective marketing videos are oftentimes funny and oftentimes very informative. It's important that videos are professional looking, even if you decide to produce them yourself. Professional videos have also been proved to work quite well along site user-generated videos, such as user reviews of products (ComScore, 2012). For example, if your online business sold kitchen knives, making a video that is showing how to care for them and having that alongside videos from users giving their opinions on the knives would likely be very effective, according to some studies.

On video marketing, professionalism is the key factor. Make sure that any videos you use have good camera work, good sound, a charismatic spokesperson and that your main points are illustrated on the screen with text. Remember to include a call to action. You can post your videos on sites such as YouTube and Daily Motion. If you get the occasional negative video review, remember that it's likely to make the good reviews more credible and attractive. You will find a comprehensive list of sites where you can post your videos at the end of this book. Remember that their policies regarding content always apply and that you should never use any copyrighted content in your videos without the express permission of the copyright owner.

FORUM MARKETING

Forum marketing involves participating in online discussion groups and working your site into the content that you post. The point of forum marketing is largely to get back-links to your site (Fleischner, 2011 p. 161). Remember that you should not be posting sales pitches in the forum posts that you make (Choose to Be Independent, Inc., 2013). You should be actively participating in the conversation. The way you promote your site is by participating on forums where the subject is relevant to your site and by putting hyper-links that will connect to your site in the signature part of your posts. You only have to create you signature line once, which you do in your profile on the forum.

If you have content on your site relevant to the topic being discussed, go ahead and link it in your reply to a post you're responding to. If you do not, it's a good idea to link to other sites—not competitor's—that will give the original poster more information on their question. This kind of actions build goodwill, credibility and makes you a valuable member of the forum.

Remember that it's better to become a member to a limited number of forums and participate in them than it is to join a large number and not participate at all (Choose to Be Independent, Inc., 2013).

Look at the PageRank of any forum that you're considering to join. The higher the PageRank, the better it is for your site. You have to make sure that any forum that you join allows you to place links in your signature. You can check the code on the page or the policies of the forum to verify that they are the types of links you want, "do follow," which are the types that search engines actually follow to the page linked (Fleischner, 2011 p. 163).

SOCIAL MEDIA MARKETING

Social media marketing probably gets more press than any other type of marketing right now. The major social media outlets have gotten their tendrils all over the web. Even on forums, social media "like" and "+1" buttons can help you get your content shared to a broader audience (Fleischner, 2011 p. 163).

Social media marketing starts right when you put up your profile. You should always include links to your website on your profile. Link to your website at your Social Media profile gives you a very valuable backlink with little effort (Fleischner, 2011 p.171).

One of the most-common issues with marketing on social media outlets is how much you want to mingle your personal life with your professional life. Facebook, for example, allows you to create personal profiles and business pages, which next topic will cover. Some experts point out that there are differences between generations in how they perceive mixing professional and personal information. Members of Generation X, for instance, are likely to be fine with blending personal and business information, while Baby Boomers may have stronger feelings about the two being kept separate (Carter & Levy, 2012). How are you going to address this is up to you and, it so happens, is also up to the social media sites themselves, in some cases.

FACEBOOK

According to CNET and Dailymail in January of 2014, Facebook has over 1.32 billion users, who are active at least once per month, and average American spends 40 minutes a day on the site.

The site continues to grow with a 14 percent jump since 2013, according to the articles. The articles further notes that the number of users who use Facebook on a daily basis is now over 829 million, an increase of 19 percent since the year before. What all these figures mean is that, essentially, Facebook is a behemoth of a marketing opportunity, but you have to use it in the right way.

BASICS

Facebook allows for the creation of profiles and pages. The main intention of Facebook Pages function is for business use. You cannot open a profile for your business (Ghimire, 2012) but you can, of course, open up a personal profile and link your business from that. The thing to remember is that business pages have fans and personal profiles have friends. You cannot invite new friends to a business page (Ghimire, 2012). You can benefit from features in your posts same with those which are available for use on a regular profile.

What Facebook offers is a way to reach out to customers that are more human than most of the advertising that you'll do for your website (Carter & Levy, 2012 p. 126). You can take a look at some of the business pages out there—or become fans of them—and you'll see that the posts tend to be a bit more casual than the voice used in advertising. The other important points that you should be very aware of when you're using Facebook as a marketing tool:

- Posting too much may result in you losing fans
- Posts will usually get kicked down a user's newsfeed quickly, so know when your demographic is likely to be looking at their pages and post at those times
- Your posts should offer something interesting to readers; so be carefull not to post just for the sake of posting
- Keep your posts positive and enthusiastic; so please don't make them personal and petty

TRACKING RESULTS

Facebook has a built-in analytics feature called Facebook Page Insights. The insights give information on how often your page is being viewed, how many people like your page, how much feedback you're getting, your views by monthly active users including people who haven't become fans of your page and more. You can access the insights page from your page. You have to go to the right of the page and look for a link labeled "View Insights" to get this information.

Demographic information is one of the most powerful features of the Facebook Insights page. Demographic data will give you information about the people who are interacting with your posts and your page. Using this information, you may find that your demographic is larger, smaller or simply quite different than you expected. Facebook users fill out their demographic information on their profiles, which means that it is generally reliable as far as accuracy is concerned (Carter & Levy, 2012 p. 192).

Pages are only part of the strategy that you should be using. According to some studies, Facebook Page posts only reach less than 20% of the fans of the page in question (Carter, UH, OH! Facebook Pages Only Reach 17% of Fans, 2012). What this figures means is that having a profile for yourself that's linked to your business site can be an excellent idea if you want to make sure that you're using Facebook appropriately. Please remember not to spam your friends with posts about your business, however, and to read the terms of service so that you're not violating them with your posts.

TWITTER

Twitter marketing mainly consists of sending out Tweets about your business, Tweets being the term for a short, Twitter distributes posts which are140-character limited . Twitter allows you to have followers, who are essentially the same as Friends on Facebook.

Twitter followers can be built up in numbers by sharing a link to your website on your profile and by sharing your Twitter handle on your website, forum signatures and other venues (Fleischner, 2011 p.173). The link on your profile is also a high-quality backlink, so you'll want to be sure to include it. The way that the hyperlink builds authority is when followers pick you up on Twitter and link to your profile (Fleischner, 2011 p.173). Remember that backlinks are vital for search engine optimization, and this is an excellent way for a powerful setup.

SENDING TWEETS

Keep the following in mind when sending Tweets:

- 140 characters isn't much, make them count
- Use link-shortening services to include links in your Tweets without consuming characters
- Calls to action and special offers make great Tweets
- Limit your Tweets to when they are useful to followers, which will give you more credibility
- Encourage users to "Retweet" the Tweets you send and offers discounts and other incentives if they do

FOLLOWERS

Try to build followers organically, meaning through your website and other SEO efforts. There are services that sell twitter followers, but remember that these followers will never be as useful to your business as the ones that follow you out of genuine interest.

GOOGLE+

Google+ is the second most popular social network in the world, with more than 340 million users as of the end of 2012 (Smith, 2013). One of the greatest advantages of Google+ is that it can work together with other features that Google offers, including Gmail, Google Calendar and so forth. The Google+ equivalent of the Facebook Likes is the +1, a button for which you can place on blogs, webpages and other web resources, and most of the packaged social media plugins for WordPress typically includes this function.

Marketing on Google+ is largely the same as it is on Facebook. Keep your posts relevant, and interesting, and don't spam people, above all, other things. One very powerful feature, however, is that Google+, obviously, is integrated with Google's search engine. Search engine integration allows you to get some great SEO benefits. For instance, by adding your real name and your email address to the content that you put online, Google can index your Google+ profile with searched engine results. This means that your name and picture show up with the search results (Zeckman, 2011). The indexing process is great for building up your branding, of course, particularly if marketing yourself as a big part of marketing your website.

It is important to remember that Google+ does tend to benefit from a bit of favoritism from the Google search engine (Zeckman, 2011). This isn't too surprising, of course, but it does give a good reason to have a Google+ profile setup and to push it heavily on blogs, pages and other publicity venues.

If you have a Gmail account or different account through Google, setting up a Google+ account is very fast and easy. Remember to include a link to your site on your profile and to verify the account so that Google gives it more weight in search engine results.

EMAIL MARKETING

Email marketing is not spam, as long as you're careful about how you use it. The most important words you need to keep in mind when using email marketing are "consent" and "unsubscribe". An email marketing recipient must have signed up for your marketing voluntarily and you must be provide your subscribers with a link on the emails you send that allows them to unsubscribe to your email marketing content. As long as you follow those two rules and don't send out too many emails, you should be able to avoid ever being labeled as a spammer.

AN EXAMPLE

Ebay offers a good example of how email marketing could be executed correctly. If you open a store on Ebay, you can encourage people to sign up for your email marketing newsletters by adding you to their Saved Sellers list. Ebay also has tools that allow you to create newsletters that are sent out to your list on a regular basis and that allow you to design your emails in a way that will display correctly in people's email boxes, which is essential for you to look professional.

UNDERSTANDING AND USING LISTS

Email lists are at the heart of all email marketing efforts. You can offer customers opportunities to sign up for your list when they visit your webpage, your blog and so forth. Make sure that you use a captcha, the images of numbers and letters that makes it impossible for spam bots to sign up for lists. You can add a form to sign up for an email list using plugins for WordPress and other readymade resources.

Consider dividing your list up into different demographics and interests. For instance, if your store sells car parts, and truck accessories, you can make a seperate list for each and give people the option to sign up for services, and products that they're interested in, and to not get any information on services, and the option to not sign up for services products that they're not interested in.

CREATING NEWSLETTERS

Unless you feel like designing your fliers and newsletters from scratch, consider using a service that provides templates for you. Constant Contact is one such company. These templates allow you to create newsletters that you can send out at specific times and to subscribed recipients. They also come with the necessary unsubscribe button that allows people to cease receiving anything from your email list, which is vital.

Email marketing can be useful, but remember that some people experience a reflexive annoyance when they receive anything in their email box that's trying to sell them something. Furthermore email marketing does not affect the SEO of your site.

WHAT IS NICHE MARKETING?

According to Merriam-Webster, one definition of a niche is a specialized market. Whenever you hear the term niche used—it's used so often that it's at risk of losing all meaning—this is what it means: a specialized market. When you launch an online business, it's easier to break down your target demographics into various niches and to craft marketing messages that appeal to them. This type of targeting based on demographics are at the heart of all niche marketing.

When you're addressing a niche market, it's imperative that you make sure to target your language directly toward them (Gordon, 2002). If you're targeting gamers, for instance, a lot of slang and tech-speak are obviously in order. If you're targeting Baby Boomers, your linguistic approach should be much different.

Each different niche will have different expectations and different needs from your products. That, in fact, is a real strength in this type of marketing. You won't have to make so many guesses as to what your clientele wants and you'll be more likely to strike upon a need that resonates with them when you buy from them.

RESEARCHING A NICHE

You must research any niche to which you intend to market. You can participate in forum discussions, social media discussions and read other company's marketing materials to get an idea of what the niche you're after is talking about and how you might appeal to them.

You may run into situations where you find nothing in terms of marketing that targets your niche. Don't mistake this as running into a free lunch, as it's not always a good thing when no one else is addressing a particular niche (Gordon, 2002). It actually mean that there isn't a lot of money to make from that niche or, conversely, it could mean that there is a possible niche out there that isn't being addressed and that you may be able to capitalize off.

GENDER DIFFERENCES

Remember that gender differences do play into your niche. Research has shown that women prefer more comprehensive content about products that they buy online (Gordon, 2002). If you're taking the time to develop great SEO content, however; you might already have filled this need with articles and blog posts about your product line.

Niche marketing simply makes it easier to successfully appeal to your audience. You might be marketing to more than one niche, but you can craft content to appeal to them all. If you had an online store with a great many different items, for instance, the item descriptions would best be written with the goal of appealing to the right type of purchaser in mind.

MOBILE APP MARKETING

Mobile apps are effective ways to market for some businesses. One of the biggest developments in this type of marketing is the fact that these devices became affordable over the past few years. Mobile apps are for smartphones and tablets and, over the coming year, the number of tablet users is expected to grow tremendously over current numbers (Kamran, 2013).

Mobile apps come in many flavors. Some of them are downloaded to and run directly on the mobile device. Others are simply shortcuts to the mobile version of the page and still others fall somewhere in between. Creating apps that run directly on mobile devices requires the assistance of a programmer. Obviously, creating apps that are shortcuts to the mobile version of your site is much faster and less expensive.

NICHES

Remember that your niche does come into play when creating mobile apps (Kamran, 2013). For example, if your niche happened to be people looking for a new home, an app that included a mortgage payment calculator might be excellent idea.

Experts are predicting that people are likely to start making expensive purchases over their mobile devices in increasing numbers (Kamran, 2013). Keep in mind that this not only addresses the need for a mobile app, but it also emphasizes how important it is to have a fully functional mobile version of your website for people who would prefer to navigate there manually rather than downloading an app.

OPERATING SYSTEMS

Android and iOS are leading mobile operating systems on the market right now. Windows Phone is also an important mobile operating system to consider. Getting your app distributed through the official venues—Google Play, iTunes, etc.—is the best way to get them noticed. There are other sites that you can distribute them on, but the official sites are more distinctive, have far more credibility and make it easy to access for people to download and install apps.

RANKING

Apps ranking system is in use many of the distribution sites. Encourage your users to rate your app so that a good app gets rewarded with a good endorsement from users. Remember that negative reviews should be viewed as useful feedback that your app may need to be changed around a bit.

CHAPTER 3

PAID MARKETING

Up until now, most of the advertising methods discussed have been free or virtually so. There is an important place for paid marketing in online business, however, because you need to spend money on this marketing, it's imperative that the choices in marketing venues are sensible ones. The aforementioned PageRank system from Google is a great way to assess the relative value of online ads. An advertising budget has to be reasonable to get a decent return on investment, so be sure you're being realistic in choosing your advertising venues. In some cases, for instance, it could be better to pay three times as much for an advertisement on a very popular and highly trafficked site then it would be to pay for 50 advertisements on websites that nobody visits.

ADVERTISEMENTS

There are several different types of online ads available. When paid advertising is being discussed, display advertising is usually what's being purchased. You also hear this referred to as banner advertising. Banner ads are for sale in predetermined sizes by the venues that offer them, with larger banners costing more. Some ad space on websites is also sold based on the frequency of the ad displayed, with several different advertisers potentially getting the same spot on a webpage at various times. The display frequency of an ads banner is oftentimes affects the overall cost of the endeavor.

BUYING ADVERTISEMENTS

CPI

CPI stands for "cost per impression". CPI is a technical term for selling an advertisement based upon the frequency with which it appears on a webpage (Wikipedia.org). The advantage in this type of advertising is that it enables you to compare the results of your advertising with the amount of money that you are paying for that advertising and adjusting the amount of spending that you are paying depending upon the value of the advertising to your business. For instance, if a venue turns out to be able to send a considerable amount of traffic to your website, you may want to increase the budget for that advertisement. If the cost per impression, however, is not justified by the amount of traffic that the advertisement is giving you, you can simply drop the advertisement and put the money to better use.

DESIGN

Some venues that sell banner advertisements can create a banner for you for an extra fee, or you can have a graphic designer create your banner. Unless you have highly developed graphic design skills, it is a good idea to have a professional handle this work for you. A small mistake can make a logo unreadable, or an advertisement very unattractive.

AFFILIATE MARKETING

Affiliate marketing is another route you may want to take to advertising your business. Affiliate marketing involves paying company that, in turn, has affiliates place links to your website on their websites, hopefully driving traffic your way. These programs can bill you in many different ways. You may end up paying for every time somebody visits your website – that is not highly advisable – or you may pay based upon the customer taking action, which is more tenable. For instance, you may pay a fee for the affiliate advertisement every time a client is referred by a particular affiliate and fills out a form signing up for an email list, buys a product or takes some other action.

The biggest selling point for affiliate marketing is quite simply that you only pay for it when you get a result (Rowse, 2009). If you're trying to keep your advertising budget manageable, but you want to make certain that you do get an advertisement for your business on a network of different websites, affiliate marketing may prove a good option for you.

PAY-PER-CLICK

Pay per click advertising is one of the most popular forms of advertising on the web. Nowadays, there are probably just a few people who run a website that haven't heard of Google Adwords. You can sign up for the Google Adwords program at:

http://www.google.com/adwords/?sourceid=awo&subid=ww-et-awhp_nelsontest3_nel_p&clickid

Pay per click advertising works based on keywords. You bid on a keyword that you want to show up for in a specialized area on search results (Google.com). You can see how this keyword system works by typing any term into Google and looking at the top and right-hand sides of the page. On the top of the actual organic search results, you'll see paid advertisements for companies that have bid on the keywords that you searched. You will also see such displays along the right side of the page.

The advantage in pay per click advertising is that with little effort it can drive a lot of traffic to your website very quickly. Another great advantage is that you only pay the amount you agreed to bid for the keyword when somebody actually clicks on the link and visits your page. On the other hand, one of the main the disadvantage is that, as soon as you drop the campaign; you stop getting results from it. This method particularly differentiates it a great deal from the search engine optimization strategies discussed in Chapter 2.

PAGERANK'S ROLE IN ADVERTISING VENUES

The Google PageRank system plays heavily into how much you're going to pay for an online ads. The higher the PageRank a site has, the higher amount of money you're going to pay for an advertisement on that venue. There is an important caveat here that you have to keep in mind.

Facebook has a very high PageRank. High PageRank may lead you to believe that purchasing a paid advertisement on Facebook would be worth every penny. There is, however, conflicting evidence about how effective advertising via paid advertisements on Facebook is. General Motors famously pulled all of their paid Facebook advertisements due to a perceived lack of effectiveness. Some authors, however, hold that there isn't quite enough data available to determine how effective Facebook paid advertising is (Gustin, 2012). Sites with very high PageRank can charge a lot of money for the ads that you run on them. Before you go ahead and spend this amount of money, make sure of the following:

- The page is known to be an effective advertising venue
- The page appeals to your target niche
- The return on investment is likely to justify the expense

Please remember there are plenty of places where you can look for information about the efficacy of advertisements on any given website. Doing a Google search is a great start.

CHAPTER 4

EVERYDAY BUSINESS INFO

In many regards, running an online business is like running any other type of business. It is crucial that you keep track of your money, make sure that you keep products that sell in stock, and get rid of ones that do not. Above all other things, make certain that you pay attention to customer service and make it your primary goal to offer outstanding customer service in every regard. There are also some practical and imperative considerations that you need to take into account that will determine whether your business succeeds or fails over the long-term.

ACCOUNTING

You do not need to be an accountant to run your own business. You do, however, need to be able to keep your books in order. Keeping the track of your orders means that you have to track your expenses, your profits and all of the other information that goes into getting an overall financial picture of your business to know whether you have succeeded or have failed

The easiest way to get started with your accounting is to arrange a meeting with an actual accountant and go over your business structure with them, discuss options for filing for other structures – LLC, corporation, etc. – and to get advice from an accountant on how you should keep your books. You should bear in mind that some these accountants will be very particular about that last part. At the end of the tax year, some accountants will ask you to hand them a spreadsheet with all of your financial information, and others may ask you a specific type of file created from a specific type of software. Below, here are listed some of the more popular software suites that you may want to consider purchasing for your company.

SOFTWARE

Quicken: Quicken is a relatively simple software that comes in versions designed for businesses. Which version you need will depend upon your business structure. If you're running your business as a sole proprietorship and you're simply counting the money you make off the business as personal income, you can likely get away with using the home version of this software. If you have more complex business needs, however, you should go ahead, and get the business version of the suite so that you have all of the relevant features you'll need to keep good records.

QuickBooks: QuickBooks is a very popular program among accountants that have advanced features suitable for business users. In some regards, it is much more complex to use than Quicken. Your accountant may very well specialize in this software as many of them do these days. If they recommend that you get this software, it probably will make it easier for you to work with them at the end of the year if you do, as you'll simply be able to send your QuickBooks data to them in its native format, and they can take It from there.

Peachtree: Peachtree is another advanced accounting software that is preferred by some accountants. It has versions available that have features that are extensive and comprehensive enough to keep good records on complex businesses.

Excel: Excel is a type of spreadsheet program available for Microsoft as part of the Office suite or as a standalone product. For the simplest businesses out there, it may provide the ideal solution for record keeping. The disadvantages of using Excel, however, include the fact that it doesn't have provisions to be set up to get the information automatically from bank accounts and add them to the ledger. You'll have to do this manually and, because many banks and other online payment venues don't keep history for an entire year, you will at least have to make certain to do this on a quarterly basis, sometimes even more frequently.

LEARNING THE SOFTWARE

You can take classes to learn the most complicated accounting software products out there. QuickBooks and Peachtree, for instance, are both products for which classes are widely available. If your accountant recommends that you utilize these products to manage your business, you may well want to take a class so that you understand what you're doing, what the various fields on the program mean, what features you need to worry about and which features you do not need to worry about.

ADDITIONAL SITE DEVELOPMENT

It's almost a given that, as your business grows, you're going to want to develop your site better so that it suits the needs of your customers more precisely. To that end, you'll need to hire a site developer or do some development yourself.

If you're intending to use a content management system such as WordPress, it's very likely that you can add new features to your website on your own. If you happen to be conducting financial transactions over the Internet, you should get a developer or security expert to take a look at anything that involves security.

COPY

As was stated in Chapter 2, content development is a crucial stage of search engine optimization. As your site grows and your business gets busier, you may find yourself not having enough time to create and add new content to your website on a regular basis. Uploading less content on your site may have a negative impact on your search engine optimization efforts.

One solution you can utilize is hiring professional writers to develop content for your site. You can do the same with professional photographers, video production companies, and so forth. The utilization process allows you to invest your money in developing new content for your site on a regular basis and to keep it fresh in the eyes of the search engine, which is one of the most crucial factors that allow you to stay visible on Google and other search engine sites.

GETTING PAID FOR ADS ON YOUR SITE

Buying ads on other websites was already discussed, but you can most certainly sell advertisements on your website. In fact, many WordPress themes are setup to make running ads on your site incredibly easy. They come with sections set aside for the traditional banner ad sizes, and, by utilizing the control panel features on the content management system, you can add and remove ads as you see fit.

Remember how important your PageRank is to the rates that you can charge for advertising. As your PageRank goes up, you will want to increase the price of your advertisements. Quite simply: sites that are viewed by Google as being more important and are given more weight in search engine results constitute better advertising products for the people who want to publicize their businesses on them. Better products are more valuable and they cost more money. If you have a high end product, you should charge more money for advertisements on it.

AFFILIATE OR NOT?

You most certainly have the option of running advertisements on your site as an affiliate marketer. In fact, when you're just starting out and your site has a long way to go as far as popularity is concerned, you may want to consider this as a viable way to make some extra income from your site.

When you're choosing an affiliate program as a partner to work with, remember that your niche needs to play into this decision (Heng, 2010). For example, if you ran a website that sold golf supplies, you would want to look for an affiliate program that appealed to that demographic. The advertisements should be things they're interested in; golf trips, for instance. The more you can get your entire site oriented toward serving the needs of a particular niche, the more successful it is likely to be.

CHAPTER 5

NOW THAT YOU'RE UP AND RUNNING

Getting a business started might be challenging, but it's nothing compared to keeping it running. You're going to need to develop some qualities as an individual and a leader to pull this off successfully, and that means that you might have to make some transformations in the way that you do things.

If you've already gotten your business set up and you're on your way, give yourself some time to enjoy the feeling. One of the secrets of successful business people is that they know when to give themselves a break and appreciate the value of what they've done thus far. Another one of their secrets is that they use their successes to propel them to even higher levels of success in the future, which you can do as well. Success needs to have meaning, however, and that means setting and achieving goals.

UNDERSTANDING THE PROCESS OF GOAL SETTING

While clichés such as "reach for the stars," "make your dreams come true" and "if you can dream it, you can do it," might sound nice, they're really not that helpful. What successful people have in common is the ability to set goals, to work toward them and to alter their tactics and strategies as they prove to be worthwhile or worthless toward achieving those goals.

Goals can be very different in nature. In the simplest terms, some are long-term, and some are short-term. They differ in other ways as well. Some goals are financial, and some are personal. Some goals are related to establishing growth within the company and some are related to increasing the overall stability of a company. All of them can have value, but all of them have to be realistic.

REALISTIC GOALS

To make sure that you don't mire yourself in failure, you should set realistic goals. For instance, if you are intending to open up an eCommerce site, setting your first goal as overtaking Amazon.com would be completely foolhardy. It would also set you up for failure, which is what you do not intend to do.

Realistic goals should be ambitious, but they should be realistically attainable goals as well (Lipman, 2013). Having a goal that is ambitious and realistic at the same time might seem like something of a contradiction, but that's not at all the case. Here's an example to clarify.

If you were an amateur runner, and you ran at the same park day after day, you'd see the same runners who use that track day in and day out. Eventually, you'd probably start looking at some of them, wishing you could match their pace or achieve their level of fitness. Now, imagine that you're 50 years old.

If you set your goal for running as being able to match the pace and fitness of some 20-somethings who use that park to run, and who are wearing shirts from a local college track team, you would be setting yourself up for almost certain failure. If you set your goal as matching the pace of someone around your age who is very fit and a fast runner, however, you would be ambitious, but not unrealistic.

Being ambitious, but not taking it to the point of being unrealistic, can help you to achieve your goals, which will keep you going and keep you motivated to set higher goals. Remember that those higher goals may turn out to be realistic once you meet one of the more attainable ones.

MILESTONES

Milestones help you to understand the long journey in terms of small increments. Creating a step by step approach is important to maintaining your morale, and to keeping you motivated. If you are only working with long-term goals, you'll find yourself wondering how far along the way you are toward achieving a goal, and may not notice the good and bad things you're doing along the way toward achieving that goal.

In order to have milestones, you have to make sure your goals have another quality that is necessary: the quality of being measurable (Lipman, 2013). Measurable goals are, in fact, the only ones that you can accomplish in a systematic way. Measurable goals have the following qualities:

- The ability to be objectively measured
- The ability to be described in concrete terms

Here's an example of how this works. Start with a goal that seems measurable but isn't. For instance: "By the end of the third quarter, we'll have beaten Competitor X." That goal might seem attainable and measurable, but it's not. What do you mean by "outperform?" Do you mean more sales? Do you mean better customer service? Do you mean faster order processing?

Now, let's try a different method. Instead of being vague, we'll be specific:

"By Quarter 3, we will have 5% more net sales than Competitor X."

That gives an attainable, measurable goal that you can work toward towards achieving. It also gives you the chance to apply the use of milestones to measure progress. For instance, one of the milestones could be getting some accounts from Competitor X and adding them to your own. There would be milestones toward reaching that goal as well. Another milestone might be improving the ordering process so that clients have fewer steps in ordering from your company than from Competitor X. Again, this is a measurable, attainable goal within a goal.

Make sure there are milestones for you to reach within the process of achieving your overall - particularly long-term goals. It's a psychological and strategic advantage.

ASSESSING FAILURE

You will fail in meeting some goals. It's inevitable but, if you look at failure correctly, you can also learn from it. Later on, we will look into more of the personal skills involved in dealing with failure, but let's look at the practical elements involved in assessing the failure to meet the goal.

First, you're going to have to think of failure in the right way. Commonly, we think of failure as an indication that we did something wrong. It may, in fact, mean that something was missing rather than that something was wrong (Hyatt, 2013).

Tracking down those missing elements that led to a failure is a huge part of turning a failure into a learning experience.

Take a look at what happened objectively. Ask yourself the following questions:

- Were all the milestones met?
- Was the strategy flexible?
- Did something about the situation change in the process?
- Was it a failure of design process or failure of leadership?

Why would you concentrate on what was missing instead of what was wrong? Because asking what was wrong starts the process of assigning blame. There may well be some blame to go around, but it doesn't necessarily encompass the most important reason that something failed. Asking what was missing changes the situation so that the question is less about blame and more about learning from the mistake and making it right (Hyatt, 2013).

While information on coping with failure is oftentimes addressed from a personal perspective, remember that there is an important practical perspective that you should take when you're examining a failure. They say on many occasions that people who've never failed have never been tested. Without failure, one has only known what it's like to be on top and never learn the lessons that truly successful people learn when they have to pick themselves up and recover from failures (Barber, 2013). The same is true of businesses. When you figure out what was missing, you can help your business to become stronger by understanding and accurately addressing that failure.

ASSESSING SUCCESS

When something goes right, it's as much of an opportunity as when something goes wrong. If you succeed in achieving a goal, you need to pay close attention to how you did it so that you can model that success in the future. There are some qualities that successful business strategies tend to share that are likely a part of your success. See if they've played into your success and how they may be utilized to the same, or greater, success in the future.

Discipline is a huge part of many successful business strategies (Finklestein, 2006). When a company focuses on its goals, measures, meets its milestones, and never loses site of what it's trying to accomplish, the results can be a spectacular success. You should always take the advantage of using of technology in achieving your goal. If there was some creativity that played a part along the way, it's a sign that you may want to incorporate that in the future.

Take a look at the spirit of your goal as well. If it fits in with the corporate culture, it's more likely to have been successful (Finklestein, 2006). The structural design of your company should take into account two crucial areas: what it seeks to foster in employees and what it seeks to deliver to customers.

Remember that goals are more likely to be successful if they're collaborative (Lipman, 2013). You're probably not the only one in your company that made a goal into a reality, so be confident in showing your appreciation for the hard work that others did. It's just good leadership and makes it worth it for your employees to keep striving.

STRATEGIES FOR TRACKING SUCCESS

If you're planning to be successful, you have to have a method of tracking your progress along the way beyond setting milestones. What you need is a kind of data that you can use to make objective measurements. Here are some methods that you can use to accomplish that.

FINANCIAL

Accounting software packages were discussed in an earlier chapter. If you want to get the most out of your accounting software, learn to use their features.

Most of them have built-in budget tracking features and other components that allow you to get great visual information on how you're doing on progress toward your goals. For instance, the program Quicken can be executed so that when you open the program it presents you with charts and graphs that enable you to see your cash flow, where it's going and how much is coming into your account. Use these types of tools to keep yourself on track and to make sure you know whether what you're doing is functioning or not.

Make sure to check your cash daily. Many successful business managers start out their day looking at the finances so that they can have an overview of how the company's doing and get information about any pressing needs that need to be met so that they can help to navigate the company in a safe direction. If you have accounting software, you have the tools that you need. Make sure you're using them! As you start to achieve more of your goals, the goalposts will change, but it's easy to change them in these programs.

Remember that the company's success financially is just as important as your own. Take a look at how you're doing personally and take a look at how the company is doing from a financial perspective. There are objective measures here that can be very useful toward determining whether you're on the right track or going astray.

PERSONAL

Tracking your personal success is a bit more complicated. The measures tend to be more subjective, but you can still use some objectivity here.

One good measure of whether or not your goals were achieved is whether or not some benefit was gained by the company. In fact, one of the ways that you can assess the usefulness of a goal is to determine whether or not it actually means anything to the company before you even start trying to meet that goal (Lipman, 2013). When your goals have benefited the company, it's likely that you can take some personal credit for having come up with an excellent goal and made it into a reality.

Did achieving your goal make you closer or more distant with your employees? Achieving consensus regarding goals is important to setting good goals (Lipman, 2013).

Take a look at how you grew from achieving your goals. You're now battle-tested and ready for more, whether you succeeded in your goal or failed.

If you failed and kept on going, you can be sure that you're reliable in that regard in the future. People who have gone through failure and have kept on going have proven themselves to be valuable (Barber, 2013), and that includes you.

If you did succeed, remember that gloating is not a good leadership quality. If you let your employees share in the success, consider yourself to have done a good thing!

When it comes to leadership, there is much to learn and many tools to take advantage of that can help you to develop the most important leadership qualities. Some people have more leadership attributes than others, but the aforementioned quality of being able to be improved by failure rather than crushed by it is among them. The next chapter will detail leadership and the qualities that make an effective leader.

CHAPTER 6

LEADERSHIP: READING AND LEADING PEOPLE

Leadership isn't an attribute that everyone is born with. You've probably heard the expression "born leader" before, but not every leader starts out as someone who not only can lead people with his ability, but who enjoys it and who gets personal satisfaction from it.

Leadership, in many cases, is a necessity, and the ability to lead arises from that necessity. You'll find that some of the most significant leadership qualities that you embody, and that you develop, are your interpersonal skills, namely your ability to understand people, to communicate the need for certain actions to be undertaken, and to communicate clear goals to people.

Learning to be a leader may be particularly challenging for you or may come easily, depending upon your disposition and your prior experience. For anybody trying to run a business, however, being able to provide good leadership is an intrinsic part of making a business successful.

WHAT DOES IT MEAN TO LEAD?

Before we get too far into the details of being a good leader, it's useful to have some definition of what a leader does. A leader is someone who can help to organize, and direct the energies of a group of people toward a common goal. A leader, in short, is someone who can take a group of people and help them to achieve things that they may not have been able to achieve on their own, and that are sometimes truly remarkable (Sprenger, 2010).

There are very different styles of leadership that you'll find throughout the business world. Some leaders are extremely demanding, sometimes downright harsh, on their employees, and if they're working with the right types of people, these leaders can get results. Other leaders are more laid-back and tend to allow people a lot of freedom, as long as the work gets done. Some leaders fall into the unpleasant category of micromanagers who, to some extent, never actually give up their old jobs and simply dictate every detail of how those jobs are done to whoever is filling that role at the moment.

Developing the appropriate skills for a leader doesn't mean that you're going to become a generic leader. You're still going to become the type of leader that your disposition inclines you to be. It is crucially important to keep in mind is that, while your leadership style may be very different from other managers you have had in the past or even other managers within your same company, there are some characteristics of good leaders that tend to be nearly universal.

COMMUNICATION

If you cannot communicate with people, you simply cannot lead them. Communications skills are some of the foundational elements of a good leader. A good leader should be able to communicate goals, communicate which efforts toward those goals are working and which are not; a good leader can communicate in ways that sometimes entails offering criticism to an employee about how they are doing their jobs, how they may improve their work and why they need to do those things.

Communication comes in many forms. Some forms of communication are not quite so obvious to people who are not introduced to the concept of leadership. For instance, communication sometimes comes in the form of a phone call or an email, but your body language and other forms of nonverbal communication can be vital tools for leaders (Adair, 2007).

As you develop your leadership skills, you're going to find that the way you communicate with employees and everyone else that you have to work with to keep your business going can be an important part of your success or failure of your business overall. You're also going to find that communication isn't always something that you intended to do. For example: telling someone that you're open to their ideas while you recline in your office chair with your arms crossed over your chest is a rather contradictory set of signals.

WORKING ON YOUR COMMUNICATION SKILLS

Your communication skills will likely become more refined as you continue your life journey as a business leader. There are basic rules that you can follow, however, to ensure that you are being as effective as possible - even if you're not absolutely certain how to get the message across.

One of the most important attributes of communication is also one that would seem the most obvious to just about anyone: clarity. Whenever you are working with a team, whether you are addressing them from a podium or at a lunch, make certain that you are always clear. The way to be certain that you are clear is to consider what you are about to say before you say it, and to make certain that whatever you say is absolutely without any vagary or ambiguity (Adair, 2007). Using vague language sets up your team for failure. When your team is not clear on what you expect of them or what their goals should be, it's unreasonable to expect them to succeed.

If you've ever read the writing of one of the most accomplished scientists in the world, such as Hawking or Einstein, you'll notice that they tend to aim for clarity in what they say. They may be explaining extremely complex concepts to people who likely have very little formal background in the subject matter being discussed, but it is their clarity that makes what they say intelligible. Whenever you're working with people in the capacity of a leader, try to avoid using technical jargon or other types of speech that confound the point you're trying to make (Adair, 2007). The clearer your language is, the more likely that people are going to understand what you're saying and be able to retain what you said.

It's also important to not overestimate your abilities as a speaker. It is perfectly acceptable – and not at all indicative of some kind of disordered personality – to talk to yourself and rehearse what you plan on saying to the people that you are leading. You can also bring along visual aids, and other aids to help people understand what you're saying and to put it into context (Adair, 2007). It is also a very good idea to spend some time talking to yourself, imagining questions that might be asked, answering them, and refining your message until it is as clear and understandable as possible. Asking questions to yourself makes it much more likely that the people you're dealing with are going to understand what you're saying, and that you'll all be able to work toward the same goal harmoniously.

HOW YOU SAY IT MATTERS

To be a good leader, you should be able to keep people's morale high. Whenever you are communicating a goal, progress toward a goal or anything else to the people with whom you work, make certain that you are doing it with some enthusiasm and with some positivity (Sprenger, 2010). When you can communicate enthusiasm for what you are telling the people that you lead, they pick up on it and, like most other human emotions, enthusiasm is contagious.

Communicating in a way that shows a lack of enthusiasm, cynicism or emotional flatness can disengage people from the work that they are doing together and can destroy people's coherence as a team. As their leader, you have to inspire people. That can be hard sometimes, but it's simply the role of anyone who is in charge of leading people toward a common goal.

COMPASSION

If your employees feel like you have absolutely no regard for their feelings and no sense of gratitude for the hard work that they have done for you already, it's not likely that you're going to get too far as a leader.

To be a good leader, you have to take into account the emotional aspects of the decisions that you make, and how they affect your employees (Sprenger, 2010). Without doing so, you can set up a situation where they feel like you are distant and removed from what is going on in their lives, and that implies that you don't really have any sense of compassion for the difficulties that they face in trying to achieve the goal set forth for them.

On some occasions, you're going to run into situations when an employee simply cannot deliver on part of a project, or when an employee becomes extremely emotional about criticism or the amount of work you expect them to do. These are normal, natural reactions for people under some circumstances, particularly those under stress.

Great leaders are generally respected for their intelligence. Part of intelligence is emotional intelligence. Emotional intelligence, to put it simply, essentially means being able to understand and react to emotions in appropriate ways. If you don't have well-developed emotional intelligence, you're probably not going to have that much success as a leader as it makes it rather difficult to work with people (Sprenger, 2010). Simply put, you have to understand and be able to react appropriately to other people's emotional cues, and you should to be able to control and use your emotions to a constructive end.

There is more to emotional intelligence than the ability to empathize with people. By understanding emotions, working to control your own, and even learning to change your own emotions, you can actually increase your ability to lead (Sprenger, 2010).

Here's a very simple – block even – example of emotional intelligence at work. Imagine that you're helping a child to learn to ride a bike, and they take a spill off of it, skinning their knee. Anybody who has ever done something like this knows that, when a child gets hurt, there's usually a second or two seconds of time in which the child is deciding how they are going to react to this. If you adopt a posture of being extremely concerned and worried, there's a good chance that the child is going to start crying. If, upon realizing that the child isn't seriously hurt at all, you start laughing, the child will follow your lead.

You will, in the capacity of a leader, run into situations where people are very upset about something and where they need to have an emotional problem addressed. The reason for this might be because they feel that their ideas are not being taken seriously, it may be that they feel that their work isn't appreciated or, in some cases, they may be dealing with a feeling of insecurity about their job. How you react to those emotions will influence how they react to their emotions.

This situation requires you to be patient. Remember that emotions sometimes come on as a huge flood of information from your brain, but they don't really reveal what they are until you take the time to consider them (Sprenger, 2010). You and just about everybody you have ever met has probably had a moment in their life when somebody asked them how they were feeling and when they really didn't know how they were feeling. Emotions are not always transparent. Understanding this is a big part of being compassionate with people. When people seem like they're about to blow their top, realize that they may not even know why.

IS COMPASSION SYMPATHY?

Take a look around the Internet for the answer to this question,

, and you'll find any number of people trying to throw in their two cents on the matter. Many of them are actually trying to sell you self-help books of some sort.

One of the hallmarks of a good manager is a reliance on reliable information. With this spirit in mind, let's take a look at the first definitions of both sympathy and compassion from the Merriam-Webster.com dictionary website.

Sympathy: an affinity, association, or relationship between persons or things wherein whatever affects one similarly affects the other Compassion: sympathetic consciousness of others' distress together with a desire to alleviate it

Despite all of the back-and-forth between various Internet philosophers as to what these two words mean, they actually do have concrete meanings. Those meanings, moreover, are closely related.

It is crucially important to pay attention to the fact that compassion does involve some degree of sympathy. The difference between the two is that, going by the Merriam-Webster definitions, sympathy is a situation in which one person is affected by something and another person is affected similarly, and compassion is a situation where there is some sympathy for what another person is going through, but there is a desire to alleviate it. That desire to alleviate it makes all the difference in the world for a leader.

Always remember how important it is to convey enthusiasm. Conveying positivity is equally important. Being compassionate to one of your employees who has hit a rough spot doesn't mean commiserating with them, and it doesn't mean accepting their assessment of the situation if it is overly negative. It merely means acknowledging that you are affected by it as well, and it also means using your abilities as a leader to help them overcome it.

Think about it this way: Great generals who have hungry troops don't sympathize to the point that they lose their morale and figure that, since everybody is hungry, they all just might as well go home. They sympathize with the hunger and then they get food for their troops. Those people who commiserate with you are oftentimes the ones who are helping you the least. Those people who sympathize with what you are going through but who also help you to understand what tools you have to overcome the hardships that you are facing are the people that genuinely inspire you. Being inspiring is a significantly important part of being a leader.

COMMITMENT

Being committed to a goal is a hallmark quality of an excellent leader. The ability to make a commitment is also a hallmark of maturity (Sprenger, 2010). When you can honestly commit to something, you develop a few qualities that make you better as a leader. These leadership qualities include:

- The ability to endure hardship
- The ability to endure disappointment
- The ability to change milestones and goals when needed
- The ability to recognize both success and failure

When you commit to something, understand that there's a difference between commitment and being bullheaded. One of the pitfalls that people sometimes fall prey to when they are trying to commit themselves to something is committing to doing something in a particular way rather than committing to reaching their goal. Sometimes, strategies and tactics have to be changed on the fly to make the goal attainable. There is a very well-known expression in the military about how plans change the instant that you encounter the enemy. This is true.

Rather than committing to doing everything in the way that you had anticipated doing it from the start, try committing to achieving the goal and being flexible in the pursuit of that goal. You'll likely find that you get a lot more mileage out of your plans and a lot more success in reaching your goals by doing so.

There are different types of commitment that a leader needs to be aware of. Some writers on the subject have broken up leadership qualities related to commitment into categories including: commitment to people, commitment to an organization, commitment to the truth, commitment to the self and commitment to leadership (Leheney, 2009). Other authors have broken up commitment in other ways, but this division is particularly useful.

Commitment to people means committing to the ways that you connect to the people you work with. Commitment to the self means committing to developing yourself more as a human being. Commitment to the organization is visible enough, and commitment to the truth, of course, means committing to being truthful, and to accepting truths, no matter how difficult either might be. Commitment to leadership means throwing yourself wholeheartedly into your role as a leader and how willing you are to embrace the behaviors that define a leader who is truly effective at what they do (Leheney, 2009).

When people make a solid commitment to something, it's easier for those around them to take that person seriously. For instance, if you regularly tell your friends that you are planning to start taking better care of yourself by exercising and quitting smoking, but you fail to do either over and over again, they're not going to take you seriously in that regard. The same is true about being a leader. If you promised the people that you are in charge of leading that you're going to do something for the project, and you don't come through, they are going to take you less seriously the next time around.

When you commit to something as a leader, it's important for you to follow through on it. There will be those occasions when you cannot follow through on something you promised, and some of those occasions will involve circumstances that are completely unavoidable. When this is the case, you'll likely find that your communication skills as a leader come into play, of course, and you'll also need to be able to utilize your skills at compassion to be able to sympathize with some of the frustration that the people you are leading will likely show.

Follow through on what you promise people. If you do, it's only going to help you as a leader.

ASSESSING YOUR LEADERSHIP QUALITIES

Here are some exercises you can do to assess how you are progressing as a leader. You may find that you excel in some of these areas and not others. You can always work on the areas where you need improvement – that's a lifetime effort for a leader, in fact – and adjust your leadership style to emphasize those qualities that you embody very well already.

YOUR ABILITY TO MOTIVATE

Take an objective look at how motivated your employees or team members are to get on with their work after you explain it to them and set them on the task. If they're ready to go right after they talk to you, you're probably doing very well in this regard.

If you're having problems getting people motivated, check whether or not you are communicating enthusiasm for the task at hand. If you come off as not particularly motivated, you cannot logically expect the people that you lead to be motivated. This is a two-way street, as was demonstrated before.

ABILITY TO INSPIRE

Sometimes you have to be able to inspire people. In fact, being able to inspire people is one of the most characteristic traits of a leader. Watch just about any movie where the plot centers on a leader, and you'll see some version of the Saint Crispin's Day speech from Henry V by Shakespeare.

Go ahead and read this speech. It's a short seminar on leadership. In the speech, Henry identifies with all of the men in his army, acknowledges the hardships that they are about to face and explains how, as people who have faced those hardships together, they will become more than most other people ever will. In this speech, he shows compassion for his men, he communicates what they should expect and what they are expected to do, and he commits to what they are about to do himself.

There is a reason this speech has become so influential in literature of all types. You will be able to see it over and over again. If there's one important lecture to take from it, take from it the fact that an inspiring leader who manages to say the right words at the right time – even if it is in a work of fiction – can become a figure who, either directly or indirectly, is remembered for centuries.

INTEGRITY

As a leader, your integrity goes a long way toward giving your team a valid reason to trust you and what you say. Your integrity describes your commitment to your values. In the context of leadership within a company, it can mean your commitment to personal values such as honesty, forthrightness, compassion and open-mindedness. It can also mean your commitment to helping your company, and loyalty to the people that you work with.

If you're not demonstrating integrity, you are just not living up to one of the most basic and fundamental aspects of leadership. Integrity is something that we learn through our experiences, and it is something that we can communicate to the people around us and encourage by example (Sprenger, 2010).

The easiest way to assess your level of integrity is to simply listen to your conscience. In a person with a healthy amount of character, and a personality that is defined by their integrity, they will generally get a very bad feeling about something they are about to do if what they are about to do conflicts with their inner sense of values or morality (Sprenger, 2010). If you have a feeling that something you are doing crosses a line, there's a good chance that it does and you may want to reassess whether or not you should take that action and whether or not that action is going to have a negative impact on how your employees view you.

TAKING OWNERSHIP

Unfortunately, power does tend to corrupt people sometimes. One of the ways you can avoid having this happen to you is to simply take ownership for the things that you do wrong, just as you would take credit for the things that you do right.

This is one of the easiest ways to inspire the people around you. When the people around you see that you have to take responsibility for the stuff that you do wrong, just as they do, that can go a long way toward helping the people around you to identify with you as a leader.

Little things can go a long way, and it is important. For example, if somebody failed to complete a milestone but the reason they failed to complete that milestone was because you didn't give them a clear enough scope of the work that they were expected to do, or you didn't present it to them in a timely manner, acknowledging that, admitting that you should've been more clear about what you expected from them, and cutting them a bit of slack can indeed go a long way toward helping that person to genuinely like you as a leader. It's amazing what people can do for a leader that they genuinely like.

If you're having trouble as a leader, take a look at what you're doing and see if there's something about the way you work with your team members that you could fix by changing yourself or your actions a little bit. Give praise where it is deserved, and make sure your criticisms are constructive. Make sure that your team members can trust you, and that they have no questions about your levels of integrity. Communicate clearly and honestly, and the sky is the limit to what you can do as a leader, and to how that can impact the success or failure of your company.

CHAPTER 7

LEADERSHIP ENHANCING : TECHNIQUES TO EXPLORE

If you were preparing to fix your house, you wouldn't think of doing it without your toolbox with you. The same is true of leadership. There are quite a few different tools out there that you can use to try to enhance your levels of leadership, and to make yourself better all around.

Not all of these tools are scientific or clinical. In a quest for self-improvement, there is room for subjective measures of efficacy. Simply because something doesn't fare very well in double-blind tests, it doesn't mean that it wouldn't necessarily work for you.

We'll start with a pretty common technique that a lot of leaders enjoy practicing. It's called NLP, which is an acronym for Neuro-Linguistic Programming. Many business leaders have found value in it and, even if its techniques and theories don't actually end up working that well for you, there is great value in being open-minded enough to explore something just to find out whether or not it could be a valuable resource for you.

WHAT IS NLP?

Neuro-Linguistic programming was developed by two men, Richard Bandler and John Grinder, in the 1970s and is based on the idea that language processes and neurologic processes are linked in a way that can be utilized to increase overall levels of performance in areas where somebody needs to improve (Wikipedia.org, 2013).

There are some controversies over the efficacy of Neuro-Linguistic Programming. Nonetheless, there is a host of books produced on the subject every year, and it remains extremely popular with people in management. Let's take a look at what Neuro-Linguistic Programming is, and how you may leverage some of its techniques to improve your management skills, and to improve your abilities as a leader.

HOW DOES IT WORK?

Neuro-Linguistic Programming is essentially designed as a means for people to better understand the workings of their own minds (NLP Secrets.com). It uses various techniques, such as anchoring, which is used to associate any motion with a particular stimuli. For instance, utilizing this technique one might learn to anchor the emotion of relaxation with a specific word. Neuro-Linguistic Programming also uses techniques such as interrupting patterns, using the power of unconscious suggestions, mirroring, and controlling behaviors through certain techniques that can be useful for people who find themselves in leadership positions (NLP Secrets.com). Let's take a look at one distinct technique called mirroring, which has some obvious applications in a leadership context.

MIRRORING

The technique of mirroring is exactly what the name implies it is. It involves mirroring the behavior of somebody that you're dealing with in very subtle ways in order to create a better rapport with them (NLP Secrets.com). The key thing to remember here is subtle. For example, you wouldn't want to mirror somebody from rural Arkansas by imitating their accent if you were from Boston, which would be downright insulting.

Mirroring people would mean paying attention to the little things they do, and doing them yourself. For example, if somebody leaned into the table to tell you something, you might lean into the table as well so that you seem more in sync with one another. This can be an effective tool for letting people know that you are genuinely paying attention to them. According to Neuro-Linguistic Programming, mirroring also tends to elicit feelings of sympathy between you and the other person (NLP Secrets.com).

As an example of why NLP theory holds that this works, examples are oftentimes made using things that are very different. For example, many people are terrified of snakes. According to some Neuro-Linguistic Programming practitioners, this is because snakes are remarkably different from human beings and because it's difficult to identify with them. These types of techniques are sometimes used as ways to help build a tolerance for objects, animals or other triggers that may induce phobic reactions in people.

There are many different techniques involved in Neuro-Linguistic Programming. There is also a tremendous amount of resources out there that you can use to learn more about this technique, and how this might be used to improve your management skills in the short term and long term.

APPLICATION AND BENEFITS

Neuro-Linguistic Programming may work for you, or it may not. One of the things that you need to keep in mind when you're trying to improve yourself as a leader, a business owner, and a person is that, in fact, you are an individual. There's nothing out there that is going to work for every person in the same way or to the same level of success. That being said, here are some of the things that people use Neuro-Linguistic Programming to help themselves overcome.

A great deal of Neuro-Linguistic Programming has to do with breaking patterns. For example, you may have started up a pattern where every time a particular client emails you, you immediately experience a stress reaction that influences how you react to that person. Breaking up detrimental patterns as a means of self-improvement is one of the central theories of Neuro-Linguistic Programming. Let's take a look at something that just about every leader is going to have to do at some point that terrifies most people: public speaking.

One of the ways that Neuro-Linguistic Programming would try to help you overcome this fear is by disassociating yourself from it (Vaknin, 2008). The idea behind this is that by getting yourself to take something of a third-person view of whatever traumatized you enough to give you the fear of public speaking, you'll be able to see it in a less frightening light.

Neuro-Linguistic Programming makes great use of imagination (Vaknin, 2008). One of the side benefits you might get from practicing this is that, quite often, good managers are very creative people, and creative people tend to be imaginative people. The more you use your imagination, the more you can learn to harness the power of your imagination to change the way you react to things, and to find creative solutions to complex problems.

If you're interested in trying to use Neuro-Linguistic Programming as a means of increasing your effectiveness as a manager and a leader, you'll find plenty of resources out there to help you do that. There are entire books made up of various techniques that you can try and, in fact, simply buying one of these books would constitute a rather low-cost investment in trying out the techniques.

If Neuro-Linguistic Programming works for you, you may notice that you don't react in predictable and negative ways to certain situations anymore, that you're not afraid of the things that used to terrify you and that you're able to overcome other hurdles to make yourself quite a bit more effective and, importantly, give yourself a feeling of personal accomplishment.

MOTIVATIONAL READING

Motivational reading will include different things for different people. Some people find motivation reading books about other people who have overcome great hardships, and other people find motivation by reading items that aren't so obviously motivational. For instance, some people who are very data-driven may find tremendous motivation by sorting through charts and graphs, and finding a pattern that allows them to think differently about a problem or situation that has been plaguing them for some time. For the purposes of understanding what types of motivational reading you may want to consume, we'll break it up into some simple categories. First, we will address those books that are written by people who specialize in producing motivational materials, then we'll take a look at some books that people find motivation in, even though they aren't specifically designed as motivational tools, and then we will look at some business-specific books that may give you great insight into how you may be able to improve your performance as a manager and your company's performance overall.

MOTIVATIONAL SPECIALISTS

When you're taking a look at motivational books, there are some real rock-star authors among the mix. One of the first that's going to come to mind for just about anybody is Stephen R. Covey. He's the author of one of the most well-known motivational books in the world, *The 7 Habits of Highly Effective People*. There are good reasons that this book sells so well.

First, it's broken up into very readable, not-too-long chapters that anybody can page through and get something out of, even if they're just taking a short break at their desk and passing their time. Second, the subtitle of Covey's current bestseller is "Powerful Lessons in Personal Change." Good motivational books tend to talk about what the reader can do for themselves. Personal change is something that, obviously, is up to the person reading the book.

Another famous book is Conscious Business by Fred Kofman. This book is another example of how effective motivational books work. Conscious Business emphasizes the idea that being conscious of your purpose, your decisions and your goals, among many other things, is an integral part of being successful at business.

When you're looking for books by people who specialize in

providing motivational reading material, look for books that empower you to do something, and that, quite often, address issues with which you are probably somewhat familiar. This medium isn't necessarily retreading old ground. Sometimes, what makes a motivational book connect with someone is that it addresses something that is well known to be a problem for many business people, but it addresses those issues in a very novel way.

OFF THE BEATEN PATH

Ironically enough, some people don't find much motivation in books about motivation. Such people look for books that give them a different perspective on something, or that offer motivational advice that isn't directly designed to inspire or move them toward a particular goal.

A good example of this would be the book *The Secret,* by Rhonda Byrne. Some of the techniques in this book fall well short of the criteria of scientific theories. What people find inspiring about this book, however, is that it is very hopeful. It asserts that you can achieve anything you want to achieve. Whether or not you find Byrne's theories to be particularly credible or worthwhile, the optimistic nature of this book itself is inspiring to a lot of people.

Some books that fall off the beaten path are hybrids of motivational books, and books that offer narratives about unusually successful people's lives. The book *Winning* is a good example of this. Written by Jack Welch, it mixes his experiences with advice about how to encourage a productive and happy workplace.

Sometimes, reading biographies can be downright motivational. One of the most praised books in recent memory is Steve Jobs by Walter Isaacson. This book is a biography of the famous Apple founder, and presents his life in the form of a very compelling narrative. One of the reasons these books can be so inspiring is because they give insight into how highly successful people work. You also get an idea of what kind of trials and tribulations these people faced and how they became successful despite all of those hardships. Steve Jobs was, quite famously, not the easiest person in the world to work with. Quite a few leadership books would have likely called into question some of his methods. He did, however, manage to lead one of the most successful businesses in the world – one that succeeded financially and remarkably, in terms of redefining entire swathes of culture.

If you're looking for motivational books to read, don't just stick to the self-help section. Look at biographies, read novels and expand your mind. For example, *Siddhartha* by Hermann Hesse, is widely considered to be one of the most inspiring stories ever written, but it doesn't have a thing to do with business. Instead, it has to do with personal transformation, which is an important thing to understand if you are in a leadership role where you are repeatedly challenged by your business, your environment, and even your team members.

BUSINESS SPECIFIC BOOKS

Just as books that aren't specifically about business can be very inspiring for people in leadership roles, books that are about business can be excellent reads all around.

One of the most widely praised books among business people

of recent years was Fooled by *Randomness: The Hidden Role of Chance in Life and in the Markets*. This book was written by Nassim Nicholas Taleb, who has extensive experience in the markets. What's really interesting about this book is how it combines mathematics and knowledge of the markets with life lessons that will be very poignant for anyone in a leadership role.

Taleb goes into great detail about how randomness plays a huge role in how people's lives turn out, even though they may not recognize it. No matter how effective you are as a leader, there will be times when things go horribly awry. Reading Taleb's book, you'll be made aware of the important fact that, sometimes, things just have to go wrong. There is a certain statistical probability that things will implode and, because of that, sometimes things will go wrong, no matter how hard you worked to make them go right.

Far from being fatalistic in how it addresses this issue, *Fooled by Randomness* should offer some genuine inspiration to people who are facing hard times. Sometimes, the reason that you didn't reach your goal or even your milestones has nothing to do with what you did or what you didn't do. It comes down to a roll of the dice and sometimes you need this reinforced to give yourself a reason to keep trying.

The Five Dysfunctions of a Team: A Leadership Fable by Patrick Lencioni is another good example of a business-specific book that could be downright inspiring to you. Lencioni has no shortage of business credentials, and this book concentrates on providing examples that help leaders to understand what might be affecting their team in a negative way. Is it outright inspirational writing? No. It's practical. It's designed to teach lessons. There is, however, a great deal of inspiration for many people in learning new things, and that is exactly what this book is designed to help people do.

You may find that, by looking at business books that tell stories that involve both failure and success, you're able to glean a lot of inspiration. For some leaders – particularly those with more of a hard-nosed approach – these types of books may be infinitely more useful than books that are specially designed to inspire. Some people aren't inspired by direct efforts at inspiration; they're inspired by being given information about how they may overcome the challenges they face on that particular day.

BUILD A LIBRARY

Go ahead and build up a library of books that you find inspirational. Learn from all of them. Don't be afraid to include books that aren't directly designed to inspire you. Some people will find their bookshelf full of tomes written by motivational speakers and other individuals who make their living trying to help people do a little bit better at whatever it is they do for a living. Other people will find their bookshelves full of novels, management manuals, and other materials from which they happen to draw inspiration. The main thing to keep in mind is that, when you're looking for materials to read, look for those things that truly inspire you and don't worry about whether or not it says it's inspirational in the reviews or on the cover.

CHAPTER 8

KEEPING IT GOING

One of the hardest things you will have to do as the leader of a business is keep your business going when things get rough. Anybody who was in business in 2007 and 2008 knows full well just how difficult it can be to keep the business going when the economy is faltering, and when it seems like nobody wants to buy your goods or services. In fact, if you lived through that period as a business owner, you're probably a lot better at what you do because of having endured that rough spot.

This chapter will give you some information on how to handle the challenges that you are going to inevitably face as a business owner. Not every day is will be profitable. Not every plan is going to work. Some plans will be completed in every exacting detail, and prove to be entirely worthless toward moving closer to a goal that you had set. Anybody can handle the good times, but handling the bad times is where the real leaders are separated from the pretenders.

HANDLING ROUGH PATCHES

Did you know that people who have been through very stressful events oftentimes report positive changes in their lives (Joseph, 2013)? What's equally impressive is the fact that most people would likely find that surprising. According to an article called "Have You Experience Posttraumatic Growth?" in Psychology Today, it's not uncommon for people to talk about traumatic events and how they actually managed to shape them as a person in a very positive way.

Realize that when your business experiences a trauma, it's also a learning experience. That's somewhat clichéd, but it's true, nonetheless. When your business goes through a hardship, so does everybody who works for that business. If you handle the rough patches correctly, you'll realize that there are opportunities to assess what went wrong and opportunities to grow.

One of the ways to handle traumatic events in business or in personal life is to make a commitment to grow from that trauma (Joseph, 2013). You may take a look at what happened, and try to think about how the hardship changed you for the better. Maybe hitting a bad spot as far as income goes helped you to be better at managing money. Maybe hiring a person who turned out to be an embezzler taught you about the value of background-checking your employees.

If you take the hard lessons that you learn as a leader in a business and transform them into opportunities to learn and make a commitment to learn from them (remember, commitment is an essential leadership characteristic), none of your failures will actually be wastes. You'll take something away from all of them, and oftentimes you'll take away quite a bit of personal strength.

One of the techniques you might want to try is changing your relationship to success and failure. In this model, instead of placing yourself between success and failure, you place yourself before failure and see failure as a stepping stone toward success (Fenton). By doing this, you're not trying so hard to avoid failure, but you see it as a natural part of your business process. Failure is inevitable. By anticipating it, you'll be very prepared to move forward when you do hit a tight spot in your business. We need to do something remarkable to change what you're doing.

REASSESSING YOUR BUSINESS

First, you need to get the idea out of your head that reassessing your business means giving up on your business. When things get tough, you may have to reassess your business model a little bit, or some of the things about your business model that might not be suitable for the realities of today.

Here's an interesting idea: Instead of trying to measure your business's viability by looking at all of your successes, look at all of your failures. Count how many times you do fail. Now, do something truly revolutionary: Set failure as a goal. Under this model, you're trying to increase your failure rate.

The idea behind this is that, by looking at how many times you fail, you'll start to notice more how many times you succeeded (Fenton). Over the long haul, it's likely that you will find that your business succeeds more than you think, and that it fails less than you think. This way of thinking can give you a different perspective on your business, and you can find some inspiration that can keep you going.

Working with inspirational materials once again, you may want to go back and review how many times successful entrepreneurs fell flat on their faces before they succeeded at something. Even in the biographies of highly successful individuals, you may find plenty of stories of how they failed. People always remember famous people for their successes. This medium can give you a skewed perspective on things.

Going even deeper than that, remember that some highly successful businesses have failed spectacularly, but not completely. For example, Apple recently released a Maps app that proved to be, to put it mildly, horrible. Apple, of course, is still doing quite well and, in no small part, that has to do with the fact that the company is capitalizing on their successes – iPhone, iPad, etc. – and moving on from their failures.

If you're worried about failing as a business, you should consider taking the time to make a very exacting assessment of what your business is doing. This period is where your business plan fits in where you need it. Business plans are designed to be living documents. Living documents can change.

Take a look at your initial business plan and see how the realities of working in your market sector have lined up with what you had anticipated when you wrote the plan. There's a chance that you'll find out your business plan actually worked better than you thought it would when you wrote it, and it's almost certain that you're going to find parts of your business plan that proved to not really match up all that well with reality. Change what doesn't function, and keep what does.

Remember, as a business leader, it is imperative that you accept responsibility for the things that you have done wrong (Zwilling, 2012). This acceptance might seem like a hard task to do, but remember that you do have to accept responsibility for your failures if you plan on learning anything from them. If you put all of the blame on your employees, your managers or anyone else within range, you're going to find that you miss out on the opportunity to take the lessons from your failures, and turn them into strengths that you can utilize in the future.

CHANGING WITH THE MARKET

The market changes with every minute. It's very crucial to keep this in mind, because if you are too inflexible with your business model, you're not likely to enjoy any degree of success. Here are some great tools that you can use to get a better idea of the market, particularly if you happen to be running an online business, where one of your principal advantages is instant and accurate access to data.

- Alexa: This site gives you information on website popularity, historical and current, at Alexa.com.
- Google AdWords: See how people are searching for the items that they want, located at Adwords. Google.com.
- BNET: Plenty of case studies to learn from at BNet.com.
- Wall Street Executive Library: At ExecutiveLibrary.com, you'll find plenty of resources to peruse and learn from.

Learning to adjust to the market can provide your business with the capability of surviving truly challenging times and, in some cases, even thriving because of those challenging times. By using the resources at Alexa, for instance, you may be able to notice changes in the patterns of how people search for particular goods or services, what websites are up-and-coming, and so forth. By doing the research and researching further into your competitors, you may be able to identify weaknesses that you can eliminate from your business model, and thereby figure out where you need to change.

ON A PERSONAL LEVEL

Did you know that the way your brain is organized is actually set up so that it can change and adapt to dynamic situations (Sprenger, 2010)? It's true; even your brain at the physiological level is designed to be able to accept change. Oftentimes, it's your ego that won't allow you to embrace change.

If something isn't working for your business, be prepared to let it go. There are periods when you just have to accept that something is not working, and that, no matter how great of an idea you thought it was, reality has proven you wrong.

As much as your brain is capable of changing when needed, it does learn a great deal about the world by recognizing patterns (Sprenger, 2010). If you notice a pattern of failure manifesting in your business, it's time to reassess what you're doing, and consider whether or not it might be time for you to fundamentally change something about your business so that you can enjoy greater levels of success. Be open-minded to seeing those patterns of failure, because they may provide you with exactly the road-map you need to make your business more successful.

NOT LETTING GOOD MONEY FOLLOW BAD

You may have heard of something called the Gambler's Fallacy. This fallacy is representative of how poorly some people understand statistics. You may want to read the aforementioned book Fooled by Randomness to get more information on how people learn to have a flawed understanding of statistics, even if they believe they understand them very well.

Central to the Gambler's Fallacy is the idea that, each time something fails, the probability of it succeeding in the future is increased. This is not true. If a business strategy fails over and over again, that does not change the overall chances that it is going to succeed in the future. This way of thinking is sometimes described as a form of magical thinking or, more accurately, it's described as a manifestation of the fact that statistics and probabilities are oftentimes counter-intuitive.

If you have an idea in your head, and you determine that it is going to be successful no matter how much the world is telling you that it's not, sometimes it's a good idea to put down the motivational books. Make sure you really think about what you're doing, and to trying to determine whether you are risking your entire business on an idea that is simply not magnificent. After all, nobody's trying to sell New Coke anymore.

CHECK YOUR EGO

When your ego gets out of control, you may find yourself in situations where you identify too much with the success or failure of your company on a personal level. There are strategies that you can use to defeat this. One of them is to practice humility (Blanchard, 2012). Practicing humility means that, for a moment, you put aside your needs and your self-awareness and realize that your business isn't necessarily about you. Your business is about making money.

One way you may be able to better understand this is to keep in mind something called the Spotlight Effect. This is a particularly detrimental aspect of human psychology if you don't keep it in check. Essentially, what it means is that you tend to view yourself as being in the spotlight. It's a very egocentric thing and it involves you, for example, believing that everybody notices your failures as much as you do and that everybody notices your successes as much as you do (Heflick, 2011).

The result of the Spotlight Effect is that you oftentimes get very incorrect impressions of how other people regard you. For example, you may have it in your head that everybody around you is going to judge you as an abject failure if your business doesn't succeed and, therefore, you may end up making very impulsive and very ill-advised leadership decisions. Desperation seldom brings about good decisions.

Remember that, as much as you are an egocentric being caught up in the experience of your life, so is everyone else. When you're thinking about your business, keep your ego in check and don't make it about you. Make it about your business.

You might feel like, as a leader; everybody on your team notices your failures far more than is the case. This situation may make you more afraid to fail than you already are. Trust in the fact that they are as caught up in their own failures as you are, and use that knowledge to allow yourself the flexibility to be open-minded, to be creative, and to risk failure to improve a unsatisfactory situation.

BE READY FOR CHALLENGES

Remember that difficult times are always coming. This is just how the world is. You will, at some point, make very tough decisions as a leader that will affect the health of your business. It may mean having to let an employee go when they have proven themselves to be detrimental to the company, even though you very much like them as a person. It may mean having to radically change your business model, even though you had a tremendous amount of ego investment in having that model of business succeed.

You should be ready to face all of these challenges. There's an old axiom about how the farther you run away from any of your problems, the farther you run away from their solutions. In many cases, this is exactly true. If you're willing to face your challenges head-on, acknowledge the fact that you may fail, and even more than that, accept the fact that failure might actually just be a step along the way to success, you'll be much better equipped to deal with what life and the markets throw at you.

There are probably a million pieces of advice you can give people as far as accepting challenges in being ready for what's out there. Expect the unexpected, be flexlble, and so forth. The main thing to take away from this is that, because change and challenges are so common, people have had plenty of time to think up those pieces of advice to give to people who came after them. Business will get rough. Ideas will fail. Money will be lost. Either you will develop the skills to cope with this, learn from this and become a better businessperson, or you will not. Exercise that leadership quality of commitment and commit to learning and growing from the challenges that you face and it's much more likely that you will be successful in business.

APPRECIATE WHAT YOU'VE BUILT

You should take the time to appreciate what you've done with your business. Even when things are very difficult, and it seems like all of your plans are pretty much in the process of failing, remember that it took a considerable amount of time and effort to get to the point where you could even implement a business plan of any sort.

When things are particularly rough, take the time to write down the things that are going well. For instance, if you're trying to break into a new market, clearly you have worked up the capital necessary to engage in new market exploration. Instead of concentrating on money that your business has lost, concentrate on the money that it's made.

The idea behind this is not to be overly optimistic – or unrealistically optimistic – about a bad situation. The idea is to give yourself a more objective picture of what's going on with your business. As was explained regarding the Spotlight Effect, human beings have a natural tendency to concentrate a great deal on their own failures and blow them out of proportion, simply because our day-to-day experiences are very egocentric. By using objective measures to take a look at what you've succeeded at already, you may find within the process the wherewithal to keep on going, keep on growing, and keep on realizing that even your worst failures are tremendous opportunities to explore, succeed, and grow as a person, a leader, and a business owner.

CONCLUSION

The greater part of being successful online is having a plan and breaking that plan up into tasks that you can complete. By looking at the various steps described above involved in getting your business going, you can see that even each of these individual steps can be broken up into smaller tasks that you need to attend to. Realize that not every one of these steps might apply to your business. For instance, if your business happens to be based around a blog, it would likely be more important for you to get high-quality links to your site than it would be to run banner advertisements on high-traffic websites.

Remember to have a plan, to look at some of the resources listed and to learn everything you can about doing business online. The online world is subject to constant and sometimes very unpredictable change. As just one example of this, Google has made changes to its search engine algorithms in the past few years that radically changed how people go about marketing their websites on the Internet. With each of these changes, however, come new opportunities, and by having a solid knowledge of what's involved in getting an online business up and running, you can extend that knowledge into the ability to adapt to any future changes that come down the road. Please take a look at the resources listed at the end of the book, which will give you a way to utilize the information you've just taken in.

BIBLIOGRAPHY

3 Rules for Niche Marketing2002

What Successful Businesses Have in Common

Develop Your Leadership Skills2007LondonKogan Page Limited

The BIG Book of NLP Techniques2008www.BookSurge.com

The Five Commitments of Leadership

What is Affiliate Marketing?2009

How to Make Money From Your Website2010

Moving from Project Management to Project Leadership: A Practical Guide to Leading Groups2010Boca Raton, FLCRC Press

The Leadership Brain for Dummies2010Hoboken, NJWiley Publishing, Inc.

Google+ for Business: 5 Things Marketing Professionals Should Know About Google+2011

SEO Made Simple, 2nd Ed.2011Amazon Digital Services

The Spotlight Effect2011

3 Tips for Overcoming Your First Failure2012

Change Experience2012

Difference Between a Page and Profile on Facebook2012

Do Facebook Ads Work?2012

Facebook® Marketing: Leveraging Facebook's Features for Your Marketing Campaigns, Third Edition2012Que

Fast Company2012

UH, OH! Facebook Pages Only Reach 17% of Fans2012

Video Markeing for Business Owners2012IWDNow Markeing

A Solid Foundation for Sound Management? Clear Objectives

Google Plus Becomes World's No. 2 Social Network After Facebook, Knocking Off Twitter2013

Have You Experienced Posttraumatic Growth?2013

Need to Know: Four Mobile App Marketing Trends for 20132013 On the Benefits of Failure

Turning Failure to Your Advantage2013

5 Secrets for Turning Failure Into Success

Choose to Be Independent, Inc.2013The 8 Do's and Don'ts of Forum Marketing

ComScore2012comScore Study Finds Professionally-Produced Video Content And User-Generated Product Videos Exhibit Strong Synergy in Driving Sales Effectiveness

Google, Inc.2009Google Does Not Use the Keywords Meta Tag in Web Ranking

Google.comGoogle Ads | AdWords

NLP Secrets.comNLP Techniques

NLP University2011What is NLP?

Wikipedia.org2013Neuro-linguistic programming

Wikipedia.orgArticle Marketing

Wikipedia.orgCost per impression

WordPress.orgMeta Tags in WordPress

REVIEW: FREE OFFER

7stepskindlefreeconsultacy101

This is pin number for your free service as mentioned on page 4 at the free offer page.

Please add this pin to the box after filling your name and email at the page

www.howtostartanonlinebusinessin7steps.com

RECOMMENDED SERVICES AND RESOURCES

ARTICLE MARKETING

EzineArticles http://www.ezinearticles.com
Suite101 http://www.suite101.com/
Helium http://www.helium.com/
ArticleDashboard http://www.articledashboard.com/
ArticleBase http://www.articlesbase.com
GoArticles http://www.goarticles.com
WebProNews http://www.webpronews.com
SearchWarp http://www.searchwarp.com
Isnare http://www.isnare.com
AmericanChronicle http://americanchronicle.com/
ArticleCity http://www.articlecity.com/
IdeaMarketers http://www.ideamarketers.com
SiteReference http://www.site-reference.com
ArticleAlley http://www.articlealley.com
TheWhir http://www.thewhir.com/find/articlecentral
ArticlesFactory http://www.articlesfactory.com
SelfGrowth http://www.selfgrowth.com/
Amazines http://www.amazines.com/
ArticleSnatch http://www.articlesnatch.com/

VIDEO MARKETING

Youtube http://www.youtube.com/
Metacafe http://www.metacafe.com/
GoogleVideo http://www.video.google.com/

Yahoo!Video http://video.yahoo.com/
Clipmoon http://www.clipmoon.com/
DailyMotion http://www.dailymotion.com/en
Vimeo http://www.vimeo.com/
Vidly http://vidly.com/
MySpaceVids http://vids.myspace.com/
Hotshare http://www.hotshare.net/bd/share/videos
Viddler http://www.viddler.com/
Flixya http://www.flixya.com/
Qik http://qik.com/
Twitvid http://www.twitvid.com/
Omnisio http://www.omnisio.com/
Yfrog http://www.yfrog.com/
Utipu http://www.utipu.com/app/
Ovi http://share.ovi.com/
Tweetube http://www.tweetube.com/
HelpfulVideo http://helpfulvideo.com/
Gawkk http://www.gawkk.com/
Shutterfly http://www.shutterfly.com/
Dropshots http://www.dropshots.com/
ShareVideosOnline http://www.sharevideosonline.net/
StashSpace http://www.stashspace.com/
Break http://www.break.com/
Vidilife http://www.vidilife.com/
Stickam http://www.stickam.com/

FORUM MARKETING

WarriorForum–200,000plusmembers
DigitalPointForum–200,000plusmembers
WAHMForum–60,000plusmembers